HARTLEPOOL IN THE 1930s

by

Douglas R.P. Ferriday

EMPIRE

WEST HARTLEPOOL   Phone: Box Office 2116   Manager's Office 3568
Managing Director: J. H. MOLE.   Manager: H. METCALF

6-15 | **MONDAY, October 13th, 1947** | **8-30**
TWICE NIGHTLY

MANNIE JAY & SYDNEY MYERS in association with HYMAN ZAHL
Proudly present **THE UNIQUE CELEBRATION REVUE**

SOLDIERS IN SKIRTS

The Laugh of a Lifetime!   A Presentation you will never forget
Played by an All Male Cast Discharged from His Majesty's Forces

Published by Hendon Publishing Co., Ltd., Hendon Mill, Nelson, Lancashire.
Text © Douglas R.P. Ferriday, 1988.
Printed by Fretwell & Cox Ltd., Goulbourne Street, Keighley, West Yorkshire, BD21 1PZ.

Introduction

The Hartlepools in the 1930s will provoke lasting memories for many people, for here was a decade of contrasts. Hartlepool like the rest of the North East was just recovering from the general strike only to be confronted by yet another tragedy — the Depression. Whole families were below the bread line for years on end with little or no hope for the foreseeable future. Some managed to join the drift south but most stayed to endure the period. By 1935 the outlook was very much brighter and the Jubilee celebrations for King George the Fifth and Queen Mary brought some light relief. Sadness followed with the death of the King and the abdication of King Edward the Eighth in 1937. The Coronation of King George the Sixth and Queen Elizabeth (now the Queen Mother) was celebrated with vigour in the twin towns. Almost every street had a party outdoors, fine weather prevailing. Every school age child received an aluminium medal complete with red, white and blue ribbon. Coronation mugs and books were also distributed.

The local economy was now gathering momentum, providing much needed employment in the shipyards, the steelworks and chemical plants of Teesside. Fuller employment meant security and weekly wages. People were able to indulge in the better things of life — housing, leisure, country and seaside and even annual holidays for some.

There are probably more happy memories of this period in Hartlepool's chequered history than any other, the 1960s running a close second.

Nearing the end of the '30s, threats were on the horizon from across the water in the form of Nazi Germany. Industry geared up to this, bringing a certain prosperity to the people of Hartlepool and with it a higher standard of living. This too was short lived, however, for in September 1939 war was declared which was to change yet again the character of the Hartlepools, never again to return to its past.

The 1930s were happy days for children, whatever problems their parents may have had, and the memories of Frank Clark and the author recall adventures and games largely unknown today, like tops and whips with the 'window breakers', cigarette card collecting, and 'knocky-down', 'Chasey', 'Hopscotch', skipping and 'Footer'. Street games were almost never ending, new ones being added from time to time; 'Knocky-nine-doors', 'Statues', 'Tiggy', 'Cappy-on' were other games of the '30s.

Some Hartlepool highlights of the 1930s include the visit of H.R.H. The Prince of Wales in 1930. The airship Graf Zeppelin passed over the town in 1931. In 1932 St Luke's Church Hall foundation stone was laid and in the same year the Queens Rink reopened for roller skating. The year 1933 saw Brierton Hospital and Claremont School built, and the Palace Theatre renamed the Gaiety.

In 1934 Sacred Heart School was built, and Cobham's Flying Circus displayed on the corner of Owton Manor Lane and Stockton Road. Thornhill School was built in 1935.

In 1936 the Majestic and Regal cinemas opened, and in 1937 The Forum followed. In the same year Egbert the Tank was scrapped, the Hippodrome Cinema closed, the Royal Electric Theatre became the Lex and Brinkburn School Foundation was laid.

During 1938 the Royal Navy recruiting office opened as did the United Bus Station and Seaton Carew Bus Station. Church Square School closed along with the Royal Vaults, Surtees Street.

Brinkburn Grammar School and the Greyhound Stadium opened during 1939. In April, West Hartlepool Airport was officially opened by the Rt. Hon. Sir Kingsley Wood. In August there were trial blackouts.

The 1940s were times of heartache, sadness, joy, pride and achievement, for these were the war years from 1939 to 1945. Air raids started almost from the beginning of the war and there were casualties throughout 1940. The Prime Minister, Winston Churchill visited the town on 31st July 1940 to boost morale.

Air raids continued through 1941–3 with much damage and many casualties throughout the town, yet life carried on in spite of the many problems and shortages. Hartlepools United were still playing. Dyke House School was opened, as was Ward Jackson Nursery, and Col. Greenwell was elected MP in 1943.

During 1944 Mr Atlee spoke from the Forum cinema. Jack London became British Heavyweight Champion. Owton Manor was converted to a public house, and prefabs were erected.

In 1945 the war ended and David Jones was elected Member of Parliament. The beaches were reopened and the war machine in the Hartlepools run down, and back came peacetime conditions. New homes, factories and leisure opportunities were to be the priority. In 1946 Grantully Nursery was built and Hartlepool Trading Estate was planned and approved. Max Lock was appointed to prepare a scheme for an entire redevelopment of the town centre.

Massive house-building programmes throughout the town with transport extensions to the new estates were planned.

German prisoners were held at Rift House and Hart. Siemans opened new factories on the trading estate at West View, and by 1947 Owton Manor estate plans were approved.

By 1948 the Max Lock plan was approved, but not acted upon until the late 1960s. There was a fire at Seaton Carew Timber Yard in 1949 and the Durham County Show was held at West Hartlepool Airport.

The Hartlepools entered the next decade with vitality and resolve, full employment and hope perhaps unequalled in its long history. Much had taken place in the 1930s and '40s which was to shape the future, yet in later years especially the 1960s and '70s, almost every aspect of life was to change yet again.

It would seem the Hartlepools is in a constant era of change. People's recollections and nostalgic memories hopefully lasting forever.

Birmingham House on the corner of Whitby Street and Musgrave Street opened in 1913 and formed part of the M. Robinson & Sons Ltd. shopping empire in West Hartlepool, Stockton-on-Tees and Leeds. The business was founded in 1875 by Matthias Robinson, who opened a small drapery shop in Lynn Street. The cafe in The Coliseum was well patronised, and will be remembered by many as a popular meeting place for morning coffee and afternoon teas. The small shop to the left is Lithgows, The Pram Shop.

Greenside in Stockton Road, Foggy Furze, a private house which was in a state of disrepair and decay. Later·it was rebuilt and opened by J.W. Cameron as the Greenside Hotel, which remains today.

In 1946 the Public Library in Clarence Road consisted of a lending library of some 30,000 volumes, a reference library of 7,000 volumes and a reading room. In addition there was a music library and a children's section. The library was considered a model public library, well arranged and tastefully laid out. Over 15,000 tickets were in use and upwards of 220,000 volumes issued annually. Now Hartlepool Central Library it is still popular with the public, and in the not-too-distant future a new library is to be built within the shopping/town centre area. The present building is listed Grade II.

Ward Jackson Park. During the war years Corporation property was, where possible, cultivated for the growing of crops as part of the war effort. In 1945 the following crops were harvested: potatoes – 200 tons; wheat – 13 tons; oats – 15 tons; barley – 15 tons; hay – 13 tons; vegetables – 50 tons.

West Hartlepool Docks and Shipyards in 1946. Church Street and the railway station are shown in the right foreground near Swainson Dock with its warehouses, one of which was the Match Factory. William Gray's shipbuilding yards and offices are in the centre. At the rear are clearly shown the timber ponds, Union Dock, Coal Dock, Jackson Dock, Central Dock and Deep Water Berth. Many of these features have long since disappeared.

High School for Girls, Eldon Grove, now demolished. Education in West Hartlepool became the responsibility of the Council under the Education Act of 1944 — nicknamed the 'Childrens Charter'. A committee was formed 'for the efficient discharge of their functions with respect to education' and consisted mainly of members of the council.

Education was organised in three stages; primary for children up to 12 years of age, secondary for 12 to 19 year-olds and further education for young persons over school age. Primary education consisted of Nursery, Infant and Junior schools; secondary had three main types — Grammar, Technical and Modern schools; and further education consisted of the Technical College, the Art School, plus evening Institute and Youth Centres.

Grantully Day Nursery in 1946. The nursery was situated in the grounds of Grantully Maternity Home, Westbourne Road, and was one of two in West Hartlepool, the other being Ward Jackson in Musgrave Street.

The Paragon Packing Co. Ltd., Greatham Street, West Hartlepool, speciality manufacturer of many household and other products, including whitewash. The EF4488 delivery vehicle is a Commer van.

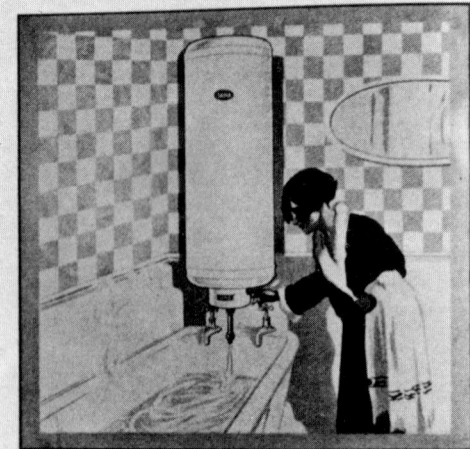

THE COUNTY BOROUGH OF WEST HARTLEPOOL.

ELECTRICITY DEPARTMENT

OFFERS

Electric
Light
Energy
Cookers
Toasters
Radiators
Installations
Curlers
Inclusive
Terms
Y not take advantage
of these and other
conveniences.

WATER HEATING BY ELECTRICITY
IS SAFETY WITH ECONOMY

Call at the Showrooms—

67, CHURCH STREET.

Telephone 2268.

HAMPTON E. BLACKISTON,
BOROUGH ELECTRICAL ENGINEER.

A 1930 advertisement by the County Borough of West Hartlepool Electricity Department. This department later became the North Eastern Electricity Board which operated from Electra House, Church Street. In 1946 the chairman of the Electricity Committee was His Worship the Mayor, Alderman Marcus Bloom, JP. The Corporation's electricity undertaking was envisaged in 1894 and power generated from Burn Road Station in 1901.

Domestic exhibition held in the Town Hall, West Hartlepool, sometime in the 1930s. The stand shown is Hartlepool's Gas and Water Co. with the very latest gas cookers on display — the envy of every housewife of the day. The lighting in the Town Hall is also gas.

York Road, West Hartlepool with gas lamps. On the left is Bruce, Moore, Pianos & Organs. York Road Methodist Church has been demolished and replaced by a modern shopping parade. The shop on the extreme right is Jackson & Dunn, ironmongers of repute, now Visions Wine Bar.

A view of Stockton Street, long before demolition and the present dual carriageway, seen from the roof of the Co-operative Central Stores *c.* 1940. The streets leading off to the right are the 'A' streets, Arthur, Albert and so on, which all lead into Brunswick Street. With a few exceptions in upper Church Street the only building left standing today is Christ Church, whose tower is seen at the top of the scene.

Hartlepool's Co-operative Society Ltd. Central Stores at the corner of Stockton Street and Park Road *c.* 1930. The store was designed by Lionel Ekins of the C.W.S. architects' department, and opened in 1915. Built of Portland stone around a framework of ferro-concrete, it featured a cupola tower. In use today, this is a Grade II listed building, possibly the finest in the Hartlepools although its future may be in some doubt.

Park Avenue, West Hartlepool. A splendid view of the Aavold Home. The whole group of buildings is now listed as of architectural interest and is within the park conservation area.

An aerial view of Dyke House School in 1945. The Gas Works is clearly shown in the background, with Steetley Magnesite Palliser works on the horizon.

Upper Church Street in 1945. Passenger transport was instituted with the introduction of a steam tram service between West Hartlepool and Hartlepool in 1884. By 1900 the system had become electrified throughout, covering some seven miles of track using twenty-one tram cars. In 1924 trolley buses were introduced on the Foggy Furze section to reach the Travellers Rest. By March 1927 all tram cars had disappeared from the streets. The year 1920 saw the introduction of the first motor omnibus services, but they failed to make money and were withdrawn. Later, in 1921, a service was introduced between Seaton Carew and Port Clarence.

The bus service grew apace and extended through the town to cover all outlying areas. The first double deck omnibuses were purchased in 1931. The last single deck trolley buses ran in 1938, these being replaced by modern double deck vehicles. At the outbreak of war nearly all buses and trolley buses were new stock and saw stirling service during the war years.

Public Assistance means different things to different people, but the Local Government Act 1929 meant that from 1st April 1930 the Public Assistance Committee of the council was to 'provide assistance for all persons who are without resources to help their physical needs'. This included medical help, as there was not a National Health Service at the time. Eventually in the late 1940s this service was to be taken over by the State. In 1946, over 500 persons and dependents were receiving monetary assistance from the committee with another 400 maintained in institutions of various types. One of these, Howbeck House, was both hospital and 'workhouse' and in 1945 it was announced, 'Inmates are now allowed out of the Institution daily'. Seventy pigs were kept at Howbeck, the sale of which raised an average profit of £650 per annum.

The Fire Station, Barnard Grove, in 1945. Records of council minutes show that in 1887 (year of Incorporation) the first fire brigade chief was appointed. In 1888 a steam fire engine was purchased to meet the requirements of a growing town. The brigade consisted of volunteers and paid firemen. The new fire station in Barnard Road was completed in 1889 at a cost of £1,225. Prior to this all the equipment was housed in a shed in the Market Yard, Lynn Street.

   Volunteer firemen were paid £2 per annum, plus 2s. 6d. for each drill, and, in addition, 4s. 0d. for the first hour and 1s. 6d. for each subsequent hour for attending fires. In 1938, after much growth and reorganisation in the previous period, the personnel consisted of two officers, ten whole time firemen and twelve retained men. By 1946 the brigade was controlled by the National Fire Service on a regional basis.

William Gray's Central Marine Engine Works at Middleton in the immediate post-war days of 1946. The famous crane landmark stood for many years as a symbol of prosperity in the towns. Thos. Richardson's engine works is on the right. Also shown is the coal staithes complex, orginally being the coal drops in the days of sail. Coal from here was transported the world over, but mainly to the Thames to fire London's power stations.

West Hartlepool Reference Library in 1946, also used as a Reading Room. A sparse but functional room, it was well used by the public as a means of obtaining knowledge and information. Today the Reference Library is still located in this room, although much improved in terms of activities and information available. The present main counter and service area is on the left of the picture near to the main windows.

The Lion Brewery of J.W. Cameron and Company seen from the air *c.* 1949. This site has been used for brewing for centuries due to the natural water spring located there, the first brewery being established in 1852 by William Waldon.

All Saints Church, Stranton, is quite prominent in the foreground as is Stranton Green. Stockton Street meanders around the churchyard to join Stockton Road, near the now demolished Bourn Hotel. In recent years the Stockton Street/Belle Vue Way dual carriageway has replaced these roads. In the background can be seen the War Memorial and the housing which is now the site of the Middleton Grange Shopping Centre.

The Council Chamber, Municipal Buildings, West Hartlepool, as it would have been in the 1930s and '40s. The mayoral and aldermanic chairs are raised above those of the councillors and officials. Later the council transferred to the new Civic Centre in Victoria Road and the Muncipal Buildings were refurbished as offices.

Birks Cafe and Commercial Hotel, Church Street, West Hartlepool. This was perhaps the most popular rendezvous for morning coffee or afternoon tea in the area. Down below in the basement were the billiard saloons for gentlemen only. The upstairs rooms were very popular also for wedding parties and receptions.

South Durham Iron & Steel Co. Ltd., North Works, during war work in the 1940s.

Ward Jackson Park as it was in 1947. The park has changed little over the years, except for maturity. In recent years the bandstand and fountain have been restored to their full glory.

The town centre looking from the north, 1948. Clearly shown are the football ground and greyhound track. The Municipal Buildings and Christ Church are in the centre, behind which are the 'A' streets. Swainson Dock is shown on the left, and is now filled in. The building in the foreground will be recognised as the Queens Rink, a popular venue for dancing as well as roller skating. Smoke from the houses hangs over the town in the background.

Church Row, Stranton, photographed around 1930, and demolished to make way for the bottling store of J.W. Cameron's Brewery. Earlier, in the late nineteenth century, Parson Rudd of All Saints, Stranton, cited Church Row in his campaign for healthier housing conditions.

The main office of Central Marine Engine Works, opened by William Gray in 1883 to complement the company's shipyards nearby. The works closed along with the yards in 1962.

The Gray Art Gallery and Museum housed a very fine conservatory, which was a haven for weary shoppers to rest in peace and quiet. Two marble statues 'Innocence' and 'Susanna and the Elders' were donated in 1930 to complete the placid scene.

Although the conservatory was demolished to make way for the new art gallery the statues have been saved and are on display in the new mini-conservatory at the rear of the building.

The Council and Officials of the County Borough of West Hartlepool with the Mayor — Alderman G.E. Hope, JP.

Typical housing of the 1940s in West Hartlepool, although it has to be said these were better than some other street houses of the period. The housing office at 10 Hart Road opened on 8th March 1946. Council houses built between 1919 and 1939 totalled 1,300, and a 'points' scheme was used for the allocation of tenants. There were bungalows for aged persons, preference being given to retired persons on low incomes. Prefabricated houses were detached bungalows provided by the government to meet the chronic housing shortage after the war. Priority was given to persons suffering from tuberculosis or ex-servicemen with serious disabilities. Special powers were operated by the government of the day to take over unoccupied properties and a number were requisitioned, put into good order and let to applicants.

The interior of Christ Church, Church Square, as it appeared in the late 1940s. The building was opened for worship in 1854, and is built of magnesium limestone cut from the New Docks in West Hartlepool. The church was later deconsecrated and scheduled as a museum in the 1970s. The building is now gutted and awaiting a new usage.

The South Durham Steel and Iron works in 1945 — settling down to post-war prosperity which was to last but a short time. It is now almost totally demolished, only the pipe mills remaining.

The Empire Theatre, Lynn Street, West Hartlepool as it appeared in 1949. The auditorium shown in the picture was 80 feet in depth and 80 feet wide and had a sliding roof for ventilation. Built in Renaissance style, it opened in 1909. Practically every stage and music hall artist of the period appeared on the Empire prior to the building being demolished in 1975 after a chequered history in its latter years.

In the 1940s Max Bygraves and Morecambe and Wise were on this stage very early in their careers. There is probably more nostalgia for this theatre than any other building in the Hartlepools.

EMPIRE LYNN STREET

WEEK COMMENCING MONDAY, MARCH 13th, 1944
5.45 — TWICE NIGHTLY — 7.45
MATINEE SATURDAY AT 2.30

SWING & SING

WITH

BILLY REID & DOROTHY SQUIRES

AND HIS

— FAMOUS — ACCORDIAN BAND

WITH

EDITH WALLINGTON

ARTHUR KNOTTO — SYDNEY BECKER — PHILIP NORTON

NICK GARDELLO	THE HENGLER BROS.	HENRY D. ADAMS
JUST A MAN ABOUT TOWN	THE TALK of the TOWN	COMEDY JUGGLER

THE TOVARICH TRIO	LILY LAPIDUS
BRILLIANT RUSSIAN EQUILIBRISTS	ASSISTED BY FRANK JARVIS — IN A KHAKI RE-UNION

Taylors. Printers. Wombwell, Yorks.

EMPIRE THEATRE

West Hartlepool

WEEK COMMENCING MONDAY, NOVEMBER 15th, 1948
6.15 — TWICE NIGHTLY — 8.30

LEAP YEAR REVELS

GIRLS, GLAMOUR and GAIETY

DAVY KAYE

THE B.B.C.'s NEW STAR COMEDIAN

HAZEL WILSON

ENGLAND'S NEW SINGING SENSATION

DON ARROL	ZENA KYNOCH
A NUT IN THE HUT	SOUBRETTE
IVOR HUGHES	HARRY RUTHERFORD
BARITONE	

LANE-HOLLEY TRIO

MUSIC WITH A DIFFERENCE

MOLLY JAMES	TONY & SHEILA
COMEDIENNE	2 SMART GIRLS
CHICK REVILL	THE LEAP YEAR LOVELIES
YOUTH, PEP AND PERSONALITY	

THE THREE KARLOFFS

EXTRAORDINARY GUYS

TAYLORS. THEATRICAL PRINTERS. WOMBWELL. YORKS.

In the 1930s and '40s electricity was provided by West Hartlepool County Borough Council and in 1946 there were 18,600 consumers in the town, having an annual revenue of £224,982. Even in those days it is noted there was a surcharge and coal charge amounting to £15,040 in total.

Many will remember Electra House in Church Street and the town being 'split' into areas of alternating current and direct current which caused great problems when choosing electrical equipment. Financial difficulties occurred in the early undertaking and, in 1905, £7,693 was collected from the rates to pay for losses. However, by 1933 the undertaking had cleared its debts and by 1946, £3,957 had been contributed to the rate fund. Output of units in 1937 was 13 million compared with 53 million in 1945, and only 48,015 in 1910. The cost of a unit in 1945 was a meagre 0.94d in old money.

Aerial view of No.2 Gas Works in 1930, which served a population of 100,000 people. The Hartlepool Gas and Water Company delivered in 1930 over 2¼ million cubic feet of gas and some 4 million gallons of water, being 45 gallons per head of population.

There were 21,000 gas consumers, 21,000 water consumers and 10,500 gas appliances hired out. Storage of water was 500 million gallons and coal used per annum 28,000 tons. Employees totalled 307. The main area of drawing water was the old quarry site in Middleton Road and an auxillary pumping station and bore hole was situated over the Howbeck Institution (now the General Hospital). The water supplied from the bore holes for domestic purposes is brilliant, pure and most potable, 'one of the purest found in nature'.

A model of West Hartlepool as proposed by Max Lock in 1948. The Grand Hotel, Binns Store, The Co-op Central Stores and Christ Church remain to this day. St John's Church, Park Road School and the Education Offices have been demolished. All other buildings are the proposed scheme. It is interesting to note the Wesley is not included, neither are the Municipal Buildings. Much of the proposed project failed to materialise except for the new shopping centre. The building at the bottom right was to be the new Civic Theatre.

Stockton Street around 1946. Trolley bus poles are to be seen in the foreground. Sutton's wet fish shop is to the left of picture. The church spire in the background is St John's, now demolished, Mason's cafe and cake shop is visible behind the single deck bus. The road is now dual carriageway and it is difficult to imagine how it was in the 1940s.

A view looking north from the tower of Christ Church, 1945. The railway station is clearly shown in the foreground with Swainson Dock in the background. Shipbuilding yards and the offices of William Gray & Co. Ltd. are also to be seen. One of these buildings stands today and is set to become the Hartlepool Maritime Museum, shown at left middle distance.

Ward Jackson Park Bowling Green photographed in 1946. The ivy-covered pavilion makes a homely scene much enjoyed by the bowlers.

St Paul's Church, Grange Road, pictured here *c.* 1930, opened in 1886 at a cost of around £5,000 and was built of plain red brick in common with contemporary churches in the town.

The popular Blacketts Department Store, formally Hill Carter, specialists in furnishings, in 1930. The store stands on the corner of Church Street and Whitby Street and today is occupied by Dovecot Salerooms.

Sage's, 6 Lynn Street, West Hartlepool: Stationer, Fancy Dealer and Bag Factor. Printing and bookbinding were undertaken and they were 'noted for Leather Goods'. The Royal Cafe and Tea Rooms are just visible next door. The Cardiff Arms public house is shown on the left.

Church Street, West Hartlepool, 1949. The Athenaeum, left of picture, was erected by public subscription in 1851, opening in 1852. Ralph Ward Jackson contributed a considerable amount to the total raised. The building had many uses, being a venue for evening classes and educational lectures, local government, and, at various times, a science school, Art College, Magistrates Court and meeting place for the Improvement Commissioners. Recently the building has been restored and refurbished inside to a high standard for use by club members and for private events. It is a Grade II listed building. The Yorkshire Penny Bank with its familiar clocks is on the right of the picture.

The Coal and Jackson Docks opened between 1845 and 1852 on wild marshlands to form the nucleus of the Dock System and West Hartlepool itself.

Ralph Spark and Sons Ltd., confectioners and caterers in Church Street, West Hartlepool, 1930. 'The shop is carried on in the usual up-to-date lines which form such a salient feature of the firms enterprise and extreme sincerity to offer not only the best quality goods, but to display and stock them in the most hygenic manner known to modern times.' The service included 'high-class bakery products, delicatessen, and other comestibles to reach the consumer in a delightfully fresh and good condition.'

Central Marine Engine Works in the late 1940s. Timber storage areas can be seen behind the shipyard of William Gray. The well-known landmark, the CMEW crane, in the middle basin dominates the area. The swing bridge over the basin entrance into the Deep Water Berth has disappeared along with almost everything in the photograph with the exception of some of the sheds in the centre, now used for storage by the Tees and Hartlepool Port Authority and Link Flow. A Graving Dock is just visible at the bottom left.

The Picture House, Stockton Street. Morning coffee and afternoon tea were served in the popular cafe. The film showing was *Hot Water* starring Harold Lloyd.

Ed. M. Alexander Ltd., The Great Tailors, Lynn Street, West Hartlepool, 'Mens suits: 63/-, 70/- and 84/'.

Church Street, a photograph taken from the tower of Christ Church in 1946. At the corner of the road leading to the railway station, left, can be seen Birks Cafe and Commercial Hotel. Opposite, on the right of picture, is the shop of Hill Carter & Co., drapers, later to become Blacketts and now Dovecot Salerooms. The impressive-looking building, at top left, is the No.2 warehouse at Swainson Dock — just behind Victoria Terrace. Much remains of Church Street today and if all goes well it will become once again a prestigious shopping area.

Edgar Phillips Ltd., electricians and plumbers, Church Street, West Hartlepool. Sandwiched in between the Yorkshire Penny Bank and the Clarence Hotel, the building received a direct hit from German bombers in 1940 and was completely destroyed, making the bank foundations so unsafe it also had to be demolished. Edgar Phillips re-established across the road where they were until recently, prior to moving again to modern commercial premises. The bank was rebuilt after the war but there still exists today the space where Edgar Phillips stood.

Telephone Exchange, Police Headquarters, West Hartlepool; the modern police force of 1946. A report of 1919 stated that the separate police forces throughout the country were 'growing more and more uniform in organisation, training and practice, and in that discipline, *esprit de corps* and conduct, which every public service should display'. The authorised strength of the Durham County Constabulary, which was responsible for the policing of West Hartlepool County Borough in 1946, was one Chief Constable and 1,118 men, and that of West Hartlepool Borough, 82 men. The Chief Constable was T.E. St. Johnston, OBE, MA.

In January 1940 the police moved into the premises in Tees Street from the old police station in Clarence Road. The estimated cost of policing West Hartlepool for the year ending 31st March 1946 was £19,500.

Cerebos Salt Co., Greatham, now absorbed into the R.H.M. complex, in the 1930s. Saxa and Cerebos table salt were produced here along with commercial and industrial salt from the brine wells scattered around the area from Greatham to Port Clarence. Salt production was later to be transferred to Cheshire, and the Greatham plant turned to many other products such as soup, chutney, baking products and Sharwood specialist foods. Today the factory produces a wide range of food products for the world wide market.

HARTLEPOOL ROVERS FOOTBALL CLUB.
DIAMOND JUBILEE, 1879—1939.
CAPTAINS OF FIRST XV's.

F. W. HUNTER
(1879–82)

W. L. OAKES
(1882–87)

A. HILL
(1887–90)

W. YEND
(1890–94)

A. J. DUNGAR
(1914–15)

W. HILL
(1922–23)

THOMAS & CO., WEST HARTLEPOOL

	T. J. WILLIAMS (1929–30)	J. O. F. HUNLEY (1930–31)	S. B. OAKS (1931–33)	J. T. WEBSTER (1927–28)	W. H. B. ALDERSON (1925–26)	
A. C. HARRISON (1933–36) (1938–39)	C. R. ALDERSON (1928–29)	H. L. LISTER (1926–27)	SIR WM. GRAY, BART. (1919–22)	C. V. FORMLAND (1923–24)	W. FRANIS (1936–38)	H. LITTLE (1924–25)
DR. W. A. ROBERTSON (1912–14)	A. G. MURRELL (1902–04)	B. S. OUGHTRED (1901–02)	R. F. OAKES (1894–1900)	F. YEOMAN (1900–01)	G. E. CARTER (1904–09)	J. V. STUDWRIGHT (1909–12)

St Hilda's Church in 1949. Flood-lighting was installed in the early 1950s. The church was started around AD 1189 by the Brus family and completed by AD 1239, although the present building is of many ages being greatly restored over the years.

One of the most interesting features is the fine Norman doorway with its chevron moulding, a style seldom found after 1130. In 1895 Reverend J.F. Hodgson said of St Hilda's Church, 'For size and sumptuous splendour of decoration, this church was wholly without a rival among the parish churches of its day'.

Croft Gardens around 1949/50 showing the early stages of planting and layout. The Borough Buildings stand out in the background, together with Middlegate — Verrill's fish and chip shop in the middle distance. Just off the picture to the right stood the home of Sir Cuthbert Sharp, historian and soldier of Hartlepool.

Hartlepool Headland as proposed by the Max Lock Plan in 1948. Gone are the older houses of character to be replaced by 'match box' houses. Very little would have remained of old Hartlepool so perhaps the public in general should be thankful the proposals never took place — what a soulless place it would have been! However, a redeeming point is the inclusion of trees on the town moor and in Brougham Street, now that *would* be an improvement to be recommended!

St Hilda's Hospital and Henry Smith's School are not shown on the model, and indeed these buildings together with a number of others including Galleys Field School have subsequently been demolished.

A view of Hartlepool, 1930. The Borough Buildings, which also housed the local police station, are prominent in the foreground. Also shown is the long covered-over new fish quay. Beyond is the Victoria Dock coal staithes with a large collier berthed. William Gray's Central Marine Engine Works is on the extreme left of the picture. Little remains today, except the Borough Buildings and the buildings next to it in Middlegate and Northgate.

Victoria Dock, Hartlepool, in its heyday of the 1930s. Many ships plied their trade, mainly colliers loading coal for the south of England.

Hartlepool Block Sands and children's paddling pool near to the Heugh Breakwater. The name 'Block Sands' originated from the site where blocks of concrete were manufactured for constructing the breakwater, and these can be clearly seen in the structure. This area was a popular spot in summer months, being sheltered from the biting north-easterly winds. The ill-fated salt water bathing pool was near by to the right.

The Council and Officials of the Borough of Hartlepool in 1930. The Mayor was Councillor Frederick J. Carr.

Hartlepool Fish Sands just before 1950, a favourite venue for young and old in the summer months. The sun seemed to shine longer in those days, but perhaps that is memory playing tricks. Certainly the sand is at a much higher level than the present day — a facility much enjoyed by the populace after the war years.

Hartlepool Headland seen from the air in 1948. Many of the houses, buildings, the coal staithes and parts of the industrial area at the top of the picture have now been demolished including St Hilda's Hospital, the Town Hall, St Hilda's Church Hall and Middlegate.

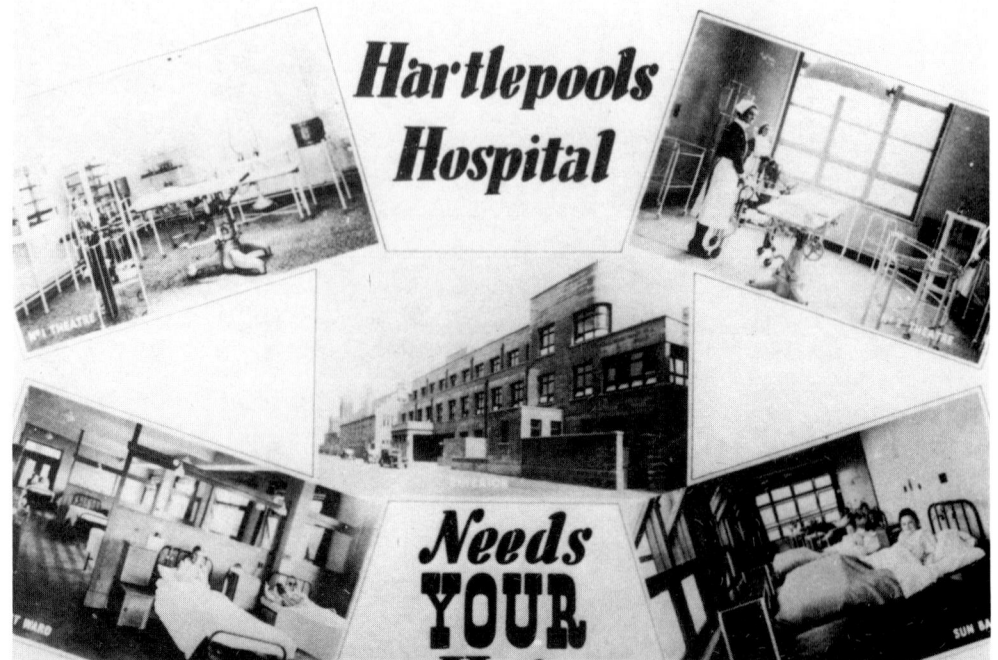

'Hartlepools Hospital Needs Your Help,' an appeal for public funds in 1949. This hospital building was completely demolished apart from the original manor house section in 1987 and the area designated for housing.

The new fish quay, Victoria Dock, around 1949. The fishing industry was still healthy, but the writing was on the wall as today it is very small compared with the past, although still important to the town. Port trade has changed from coal, timber, iron ore and fishing to paper products and cars.

Several small boat groups use the port and this should form a basis for a marina of national significance within the next few years.

Fisher wives in jocular mood, although this may be connected with Carnival week rather than the serious business of fishing.

Hartlepool open air sea water bathing pool in 1949, a very popular venue for local people in the summer but rather chilly in winter. Many youngsters learned to swim in this pool. The pool was destroyed during the great storm of 1953, but there is a possibility that it may be restored, on a limited scale at first, to provide a local amenity once again for this most historic area of Hartlepool.

Seaton Carew Swimming Baths in the late 1930s. Opened in 1914 by the benefactor Sir William Gray, the baths fells into decay and were demolished in the 1970s when the Mill House Swimming Pool was opened. The site now forms part of a summer car park.